technology of the
ancient world

the history of technology

technology of the ancient world

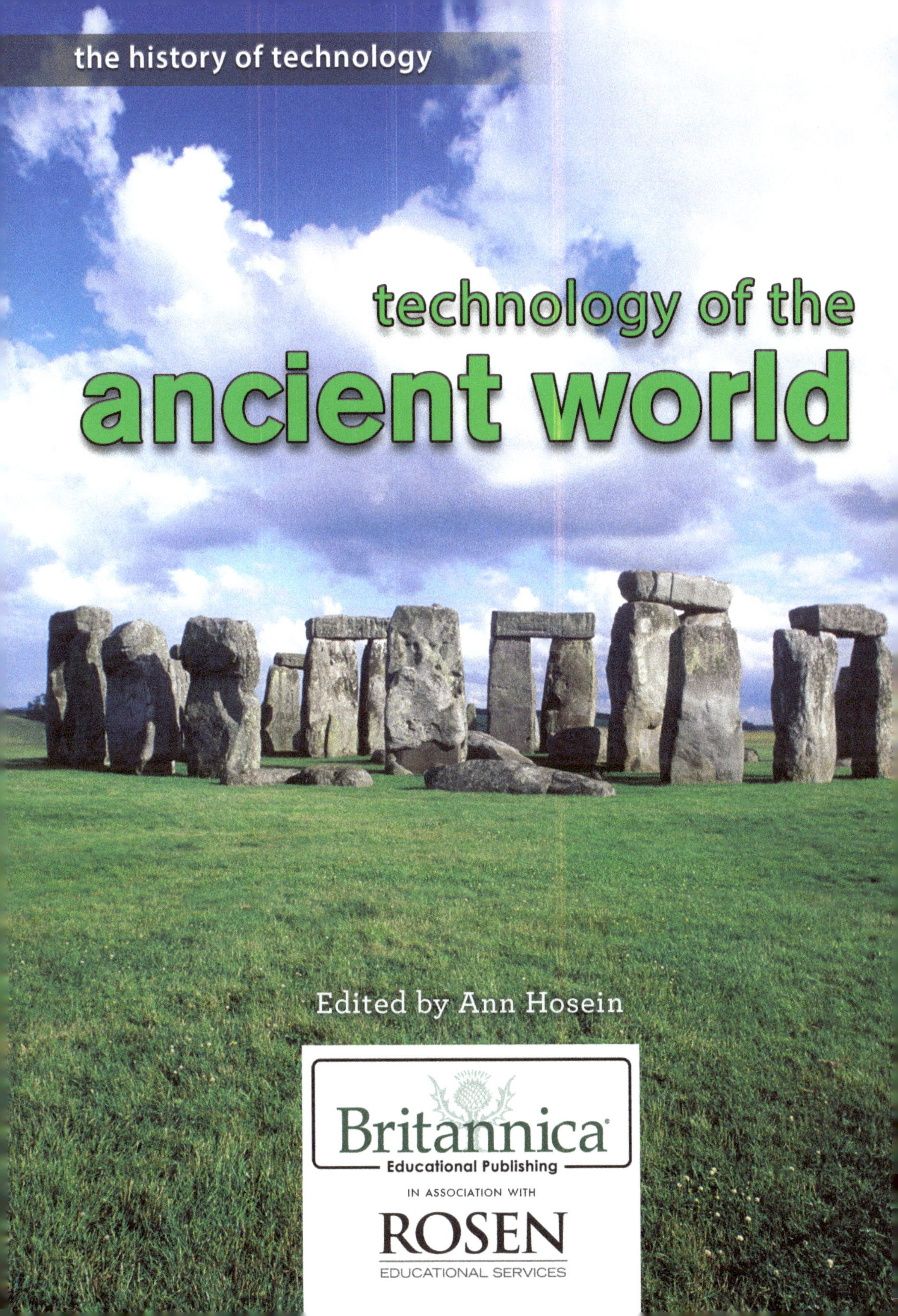

Edited by Ann Hosein

Britannica Educational Publishing

IN ASSOCIATION WITH

ROSEN EDUCATIONAL SERVICES

Published in 2016 by Britannica Educational Publishing (a trademark of Encyclopædia Britannica, Inc.) in association with The Rosen Publishing Group, Inc.
29 East 21st Street, New York, NY 10010

Distributed exclusively by Rosen Publishing.
To see additional Britannica Educational Publishing titles, go to rosenpublishing.com.

First Edition

Britannica Educational Publishing
J.E. Luebering: Director, Core Reference Group
Anthony L. Green: Editor, Compton's by Britannica

Rosen Publishing
Ann Hosein: Editor
Nelson Sá: Art Director
Nicole Russo: Designer
Cindy Reiman: Photography Manager
Nicole Baker: Photo Researcher
Introduction and supplementary material by Susan Meyer.

Library of Congress Cataloging-in-Publication Data

Hosein, Ann.
Technology of the ancient world / edited by Ann Hosein.
pages cm. -- (The history of technology)
Includes bibliographical references and index.
ISBN 978-1-68048-273-7 (library bound)
1. Technology--History--Juvenile literature. I. Title.

T48.H7375 2015
609'.01--dc23

2015017710

Manufactured in the United States of America

Photo credits: Cover, p. 3 Neil Holmes/Photolibrary/Getty Images; pp. 5, 36 David Greedy/Lonely Planet Images/Getty Images; pp. 6, 58-59, 64-65 DEA/G. Sioen/De Agostini/Getty Images; pp. 9, 19, 45 DEA/G. Dagli Orti/De Agostini Getty Images; pp. 13, 84, 91 DEA/A. Dagli Orti/De Agostini/Getty Images; p. 22 Courtesy of M.J. O'Kelly; p. 23 DEA/A. De Gregorio/De Agostini/Getty Images; pp. 26, 66-67, 87, 89 De Agostini Picture Library/Getty Images; pp 29, 32-33 DEA/G. Nimatallah/De Agostini/Getty Images; pp. 38-39 Danita Delimont/Gallo Images/Getty Images; pp. 42-43 Tibor Bognar/Photononstop/Getty Images; pp. 48-49 David Pedre/E+/Getty Images; pp. 52, 74 Science & Society Picture Library/Getty Images; p.. 54-55 Fabrizio Romagnoli/EyeEm/Getty Images; p. 56 Universal History Archive/UIG/Getty Images; p. 60 Keystone-France/Gamma-Keystone/Getty Images; p. 63 Jean-Dominique Lajoux; p. 69 Dorling Kindersley/Getty Images; pp. 78-79 PHAS/ Universal Images Group/Getty Images; p. 83 Ackland Art Museum, The University of North Carolina at Chapel Hill/Art Resource, NY; p. 97 DEA/C. Bevilacqua/ De Agostini Getty Images; p. 101 David Ionut/Shutterstock.com; interior pages background texture David M. Schrader/Shutterstock.com

Contents

Introduction

The contemporary understanding of "technology" usually refers to advances in highly technical industries such as those related to computers, telecommunications, and the Internet. Modern technology is constantly evolving, with each new advance making older versions outmoded and eventually obsolete. To understand the technology of the ancient world, as it is discussed in this book, the word must be thought of somewhat differently. At its core, technology is the application of knowledge to manipulate one's environment and achieve a specific practical purpose. Working from this definition, many basic tools that people take for granted today were once revolutionary technologies.

The earliest technology was developed when human beings realized they could sharpen rocks and bones to improve their usability. This led to the creation of simple tools, such as stone axes and arrow tips. Hunting became easier and meat more abundant, which naturally led to a need to preserve the game by cooking it. This need was met when humans learned to harness fire. Hunting provided food, and following game defined the lives and social structure of humans until they developed and refined the principles of agriculture, transforming nomadic hunters into farmers. Two-wheeled carts were invented in

Mesopotamia (now Iraq) in about 3500 BCE. The yoke allowed draft animals to pull plows and wagons. Likewise, reed boats, canoes, and wooden rafts made river and coastal trade possible. Another Mesopotamian creation was the first form of writing—inscribing marks in soft clay, in a process called cuneiform. Now technologies could be recorded and more quickly disseminated.

4th century BCE harpoons used for fishing

Each advance in technology led to further technological needs. Effective farming and transportation allowed for a denser population, and after about 3500 BCE cities began to grow. The Stone Age was followed by the Bronze Age in about 3000 BCE when humans discovered that copper, repeatedly hammered and put into a fire, would not crack, which preceded the discovery that alloys of tin and copper produced a strong and malleable bronze that could be used for swords and sickles. Mining, metalworking, and trade brought wealth to the newly formed cities and with it a change in the social structure. Armies were needed to defend and sometimes conquer new home territories. Construction of fortifications, public structures, waterworks, and dams formed the beginnings of engineering.

This book examines the technology of the ancient world from the foundational advances of Stone Age hominids to the mastery of iron work and the construction of aqueducts in ancient Greece and Rome. It studies technologies developed for military defense and supremacy, as well as those related to the production of food from Europe to the Indian subcontinent. It also considers the leaps in technological innovation accompanying the change from a widespread population to tightly settled urban centers.

Ultimately, the long history of technology shows the many ways that human ingenuity has triumphed over environment and continues to build on past successes. From simple tools to complex processes and machines, humans will forever be improving on past breakthroughs to refine their lives and livelihoods.

Chapter 1

STONE AGE TECHNOLOGY

The identification of the history of technology with the history of humanlike species does not help in fixing a precise point for its origin because the estimates of prehistorians and anthropologists concerning the emergence of human species vary so widely. Animals occasionally use natural tools such as sticks or stones, and the ancestors of humans doubtless did the same for hundreds of millennia before the first giant step of fashioning their own tools. Even then it was an interminable time before they put such toolmaking on a regular basis, and still more aeons passed as they arrived at the successive stages of standardizing their simple stone choppers and pounders and of manufacturing them—that is, providing sites and assigning specialists to the work. A degree of specialization in toolmaking

Arrow points and spearheads excavated from the Czech Republic

was achieved by the time of the Neanderthals (70,000 BCE); more-advanced tools, requiring assemblage of head and haft, were produced by Cro-Magnons (perhaps as early as 35,000 BCE); while the application of mechanical principles was achieved by pottery-making Neolithic (New Stone Age; 6000 BCE) and Metal Age peoples (about 3000 BCE).

EARLIEST COMMUNITIES

For all except approximately the past 10,000 years, humans lived almost entirely in small nomadic communities dependent for survival on their skills in gathering food, hunting and fishing, and avoiding predators. It is reasonable to suppose that most of these communities developed in tropical latitudes, especially in Africa, where climatic conditions are most favourable to a creature with such poor bodily protection as humans have. It is also reasonable to suppose that tribes moved out thence into the subtropical regions and eventually into the landmass of Eurasia, although their colonization of this region must have been severely limited by the successive periods of glaciation, which rendered large parts of it inhospitable and even uninhabitable, even though humankind has shown remarkable versatility in adapting to such unfavorable conditions.

THE NEOLITHIC REVOLUTION

Toward the end of the last ice age, some 15,000 to 20,000 years ago, a few of the communities that were most favoured by geography and climate began to make the transition from the long period of Paleolithic, or Old Stone Age, savagery to a more settled way of life depending on animal husbandry and agriculture. This period of transition, the Neolithic Period, or New Stone Age, led eventually to a marked rise in population, to a growth in the size of communities, and to the beginnings of town life. It is sometimes referred to as the Neolithic Revolution because the speed of technological innovation increased so greatly and human social and political organization underwent a corresponding increase in complexity. To understand the beginnings of technology, it is thus necessary to survey developments from the Old Stone Age through the New Stone Age down to the emergence of the first urban civilizations about 3000 BCE.

STONE

The material that gives its name and a technological unity to these periods of prehistory is stone. Though it may be assumed that primitive humans used other materials such as wood, bone, fur, leaves, and grasses before they mastered the use of stone, apart from bone antlers, presumably used as picks in flint mines and elsewhere, and other fragments of bone implements, none of these has survived. The stone tools of early humans, on the other hand, have survived in surprising abundance, and over the many millennia of prehistory important advances in technique were made in the use of stone. Stones became tools only when they were shaped deliberately for specific purposes, and, for this to be done efficiently, suitable hard and fine-grained stones had to be found and means devised for shaping them and particularly for putting a cutting edge on them. Flint became a very popular stone for this purpose, although fine sandstones and certain volcanic rocks were also widely used. There is much Paleolithic evidence of skill in flaking and polishing stones to make scraping and cutting tools. These early tools were held in the hand, but gradually ways of protecting the hand from sharp edges on the stone, at first by wrapping one end in fur or grass or setting it in a wooden handle, were devised. Much later the technique of fixing the stone head to a haft converted these hand tools into more versatile tools and weapons.

With the widening mastery of the material world in the Neolithic Period, other substances were brought into service, such as clay for pottery and brick, and increasing competence in handling textile raw materials led to the creation of the first woven fabrics to take the place of animal skins. About the same time, curiosity about the behavior of metallic oxides in the presence of fire promoted one of the most significant technological innovations of all time and marked the succession from the Stone Age to the Metal Age.

Power

The use of fire was another basic technique mastered at some unknown time in the Old Stone Age. The discovery that fire could be tamed and controlled and the further discovery that a fire could be generated by persistent friction between two dry wooden surfaces were momentous. Fire was the most important contribution of prehistory to power technology, although little power was obtained directly from fire except as defense against wild animals. For the most part, prehistoric communities remained completely dependent upon manpower, but, in making the transition to a more settled pattern of life in the New Stone Age, they began to derive some power from animals that had been domesticated. It also seems likely that by the end of prehistoric times the sail had emerged as a means of harnessing the wind for small boats, beginning a long sequence of developments in marine transport.

Tools and Weapons

The basic tools of prehistoric peoples were determined by the materials at their disposal. But once they had acquired the techniques of working stone, they were resourceful in devising tools and weapons with points and barbs. Thus, the stone-headed spear, the harpoon, and the arrow all came into widespread use. The spear was given increased impetus by the spear-thrower, a notched pole that gave a sling effect. The bow and arrow were an even more effective combination, the use of which is clearly demonstrated in the earliest "documentary" evidence in the history of technology, the cave paintings of southern France and northern Spain, which depict the bow being used in hunting. The ingenuity of these primitive hunters is also shown in their slings, throwing-sticks (the boomerang of the Australian Aborigines is a remarkable surviving example), blowguns, bird snares, fish and animal traps, and nets. These tools did not evolve uniformly,

Examples of Neolithic axes from Sweden

as each primitive community developed only those instruments that were most suitable for its own specialized purposes, but all were in use by the end of the Stone Age. In addition, the Neolithic Revolution had contributed some important new tools that were not primarily concerned with hunting. These were the first mechanical applications of rotary action in the shape of the potter's wheel, the bow drill, the pole lathe, and the wheel itself. It is not possible to be sure when these significant devices were invented, but their presence in the early urban civilizations suggests some continuity with the late Neolithic Period. The potter's wheel, driven by kicks from the operator, and the wheels of early vehicles both gave continuous rotary movement in one direction. The drill and the lathe, on the other hand, were derived from the bow and had the effect of spinning the drill piece or the workpiece first in one direction and then in the other.

Developments in food production brought further refinements in tools. The processes of food production in Paleolithic times were simple, consisting of gathering, hunting, and fishing. If these methods proved inadequate to sustain a community, it moved to better hunting grounds or perished. With the onset of the Neolithic Revolution, new food-producing skills were devised to serve the needs of agriculture and animal husbandry. Digging sticks and the first crude plows, stone sickles, querns that ground grain by friction between two stones and, most complicated of all, irrigation techniques for keeping the ground watered and fertile—all these became well established in the great subtropical river valleys of Egypt and Mesopotamia in the millennia before 3000 BCE.

Building Techniques

Prehistoric building techniques also underwent significant developments in the Neolithic Revolution. Nothing is known of the building ability of Paleolithic peoples beyond what can be inferred from a few fragments of stone shelters, but in the New Stone Age some impressive structures were erected, primarily tombs and burial mounds and other religious edifices, but also, toward the end of the period, domestic housing in which sun-dried brick was first used. In northern Europe, where the Neolithic transformation began later than around the eastern Mediterranean and lasted longer, huge stone monuments, of which Stonehenge in England is the outstanding example, still bear eloquent testimony to the technical skill, not

Entrance stone to a tomb, County Meath, Ireland c. 3200 BC

to mention the imagination and mathematical competence, of the later Stone Age societies.

Manufacturing

The manufacturing industry had its origin in the New Stone Age, with the application of techniques for grinding corn, baking clay, spinning and weaving textiles, and also, it seems likely, for dyeing, fermenting, and distilling. Some evidence for all these processes can be derived from archaeological findings, and

A Bronze Age votive from the province of Vercelli, Italy

some of them at least were developing into specialized crafts by the time the first urban civilizations appeared. In the same way, the early metalworkers were beginning to acquire the techniques of extracting and working the softer metals, gold, silver, copper, and tin, that were to make their successors a select class of craftsmen. All these incipient fields of specialization, moreover, implied developing trade between different communities and regions, and again the archaeological evidence of the transfer of manufactured products in the later Stone Age is impressive. Flint arrowheads of particular types, for example, can be found widely dispersed over Europe, and the implication of a common locus of manufacture for each is strong.

Such transmission suggests improving facilities for transport and communication. Paleolithic people presumably depended entirely on their own feet, and this remained the normal mode of transport throughout the Stone Age. Domestication of the ox, the donkey, and the camel undoubtedly brought some help, although difficulties in harnessing the horse long delayed its effective use. The dugout canoe and the birch-bark canoe demonstrated the potential of water transport, and, again, there is some evidence that the sail had already appeared by the end of the New Stone Age.

It is notable that the developments so far described in human prehistory took place over a long period of time, compared with the 5,000 years of recorded history, and that they took place first in very small areas of the Earth's surface and involved populations minute by modern criteria. The Neolithic Revolution occurred first in those parts of the world with an unusual combination of qualities: a warm climate, encouraging rapid crop growth, and an annual cycle of flooding that naturally regenerated the fertility of the land. On the Eurasian-African landmass such conditions occur only in Egypt, Mesopotamia, northern India, and some of the great river valleys of China. It was there, then, that men and women of the New Stone Age were stimulated to develop and apply new techniques of agriculture, animal husbandry, irrigation, and manufacture, and it was there that their enterprise was rewarded by increasing productivity, which encouraged the growth of population and triggered a succession of sociopolitical changes that converted the settled Neolithic communities into the first civilizations. Elsewhere the stimulus to technological innovation was lacking or was unrewarded so that those areas had to await the transmission of technical expertise from the more highly favoured areas. Herein is rooted the separation

TECHNOLOGY AND HUMAN PHYSICAL DEVELOPMENT

The development of technology has affected the selective forces that have shaped the human form. The first of these technologies, fire, made it possible for humans to live in colder climates, thereby making thawing food and cooking

What fishing in the Paleolithic Period may have looked like

a necessity. Cooked food meant less chewing and eventually led to mutations in facial structure, reducing jaw and tooth size.

The spear led to the modification of the body from the neck down. This innovation, which has been traced to Africa, meant that the hunter did not literally have to come to grips with prey and could impale it from a distance. The consequence was a reduction of muscularity and robustness in the body below the neck. This change spread northward as far as Israel. However, as cooking technology had not yet spread south, changes in tooth and jaw size and body muscularity did not occur in all human populations at the same time. When cooking technology eventually spread southward, jaw and tooth reduction proceeded in a fashion parallel to what had been going on in the north for the previous 100,000 years or more. Projectile technology was adopted by the people of the north, and in comparable fashion, the result was the reduction in arm and shoulder robustness over the course of time.

The invention of string and the use of nooses, snares, and nets resulted in an increase in food, which dramatically increased population size and density.

of the great world civilizations, for while the Egyptian and Mesopotamian civilizations spread their influence westward through the Mediterranean and Europe, those of India and China were limited by geographical barriers to their own hinterlands, which, although vast, were largely isolated from the mainstream of Western technological progress.

Chapter 2

THE URBAN REVOLUTION

The technological change so far described took place very slowly over a long period of time, in response to only the most basic social needs, the search for food and shelter, and with few social resources available for any activity other than the fulfillment of these needs. About 5,000 years ago, however, a momentous cultural transition began to take place in a few well-favoured geographical situations. It generated new needs and resources and was accompanied by a significant increase in technological innovation. It was the beginning of the invention of the city.

CRAFTSMEN AND SCIENTISTS

The accumulated agricultural skill of the New Stone Age had made possible a growth

Bronze Age gold diadem from Madrid, Spain

in population, and the larger population in turn created a need for the products of specialized craftsmen in a wide range of commodities. These craftsmen included a number of metalworkers, first those treating metals that could be easily obtained in metallic form and particularly the soft metals, such as gold and copper, which could be fashioned by beating. Then came the discovery of the possibility of extracting certain metals from the ores in which they generally occur. Probably the first such material to be used was the carbonate of copper known as malachite, then already in use as a cosmetic and easily reduced to copper in a strong fire. It is impossible to be precise about the time and place of this discovery, but its consequences were tremendous. It led to the search for other metallic ores, to the development of metallurgy, to the encouragement of trade in order to secure specific metals, and to the further development of specialist skills. It contributed substantially to the emergence of urban societies, as it relied heavily upon trade and manufacturing industries, and thus to the rise of the first civilizations. The Stone Age gave way to the early Metal Age, and a new epoch in the story of humankind had begun.

By fairly general consent, civilization consists of a large society with a common culture, settled communities, and sophisticated institutions, all of which presuppose a mastery of elementary literacy and numeration. Mastery of the civilized arts was a minority pursuit in the early civilizations, in all probability the carefully guarded possession of a priestly caste. The very existence of these skills, however, even in the hands of a small minority of the population, is significant because they made available a facility for recording and transmitting information that greatly enlarged the scope for innovation and speculative thought.

Hitherto, technology had existed without the benefit of science, but, by the time of the first Sumerian astronomers, who plotted the motion of the heavenly bodies with remarkable accuracy and based calculations about the calendar and irrigation systems upon their observations, the possibility of a creative relationship between science and technology had appeared. The first fruits of this relationship appeared in greatly improved abilities to measure land, weigh, and keep time, all practical techniques, essential to any complex society, and inconceivable without literacy and the beginnings of scientific observation. With the emergence of these skills in the 3rd millennium BCE, the first civilizations arose in the valleys of the Nile and of the Tigris-Euphrates.

COPPER AND BRONZE

The fact that the era of the early civilizations coincides with the technological classification of the Copper and Bronze ages is a clue to the technological basis of these societies. The softness of copper, gold, and silver made

Bronze Age spearheads from Canatello, Italy

it inevitable that they should be the first to be worked, but archaeologists now seem to agree that there was no true "Copper Age," except perhaps for a short period at the beginning of Egyptian civilization, because the very softness of that metal limited its utility for everything except decoration or coinage. Attention was thus given early to means of hardening copper to make satisfactory tools and weapons. The reduction of mixed metallic ores probably led to the discovery of alloying, whereby copper was fused with other metals to make bronze. Several bronzes were made, including some containing lead, antimony, and arsenic, but by far the most popular and widespread was that of copper and tin in proportions of about 10 to one. This was a hard yellowish metal that could be melted and cast into the shape required. The bronzesmiths took over from the coppersmiths and goldsmiths the technique of heating the metal in a crucible over a strong fire and casting it into simple clay or stone molds to make axheads or spearheads or other solid shapes. For the crafting of hollow vessels or sculpture, they devised the so-called cire perdue technique, in which the shape to be molded is formed in wax and set in clay, the wax then being melted and drained out to leave a cavity into which the molten metal is poured.

Bronze became the most important material of the early civilizations, and elaborate arrangements were made to ensure a continuous supply of it. Metals were scarce in the alluvial river valleys where civilization developed and therefore had to be imported. This need led to complicated trading relationships and mining operations at great distances from the homeland. Tin presented a particularly severe problem, as it was in short supply throughout the Middle East. The Bronze Age civilizations were compelled to search far beyond their own frontiers for sources of the metal, and in the process knowledge of the civilized arts was gradually transmitted westward along the developing Mediterranean trade routes.

In most aspects other than the use of metals, the transition from the technology of the New Stone Age to that of early civilizations was fairly gradual, although there was a general increase in competence as specialized skills became more clearly defined, and in techniques of building there were enormous increases in the scale of enterprises. There were no great innovations in power technology, but important improvements were made in the construction of furnaces and kilns in response to the requirements of the metalworkers and potters and of new artisans such as glassworkers. Also, the sailing ship assumed a definitive shape, progressing from a vessel with a small sail rigged in its bows and suitable only for sailing before the prevailing wind up the Nile River, into the substantial ocean-going ship of the later Egyptian dynasties, with a large rectangular sail rigged amidships. Egyptian and Phoenician ships of this type could sail before the wind and across the wind, but for making headway into the wind they had to resort to manpower. Nevertheless, they accomplished remarkable feats of navigation, sailing the length of the Mediterranean and even passing through the Pillars of Hercules into the Atlantic.

THE LOST-WAX PROCESS

The lost-wax process, also called cire-perdue, is a method of metal casting in which a molten metal is poured into a mold that has been created by means of a wax model. Once the mold is made, the wax model is melted and drained away. A hollow core can be effected by the introduction of a heat-proof core that prevents the molten metal from totally filling the mold. Common on every continent except Australia, the lost-wax method dates from the 3rd millennium BCE and has sustained few changes since then.

Clay mold of a Hindu figure that was used with the lost-wax technique

To cast a clay model in bronze, a mold is made from the model, and the inside of this negative mold is brushed with melted wax to the desired thickness of the final bronze. After removal of the mold, the resultant wax shell is filled with a heat-resistant mixture. Wax tubes, which provide ducts for pouring bronze during casting and vents for the noxious gases produced in the process, are fitted to the outside of the wax shell, which may be modeled or adjusted by the artist. Metal pins are hammered through the shell into the core to secure it. Next, the prepared wax shell is completely covered in layers of heat-resistant plaster, and the whole is inverted and placed in an oven. During heating, the plaster dries and the wax runs out through the ducts created by the wax tubes. The plaster mold is then packed in sand, and molten bronze is poured through the ducts, filling the space left by the wax. When cool, the outer plaster and core are removed, and the bronze may receive finishing touches.

IRRIGATION

Techniques of food production also showed many improvements over Neolithic methods, including one outstanding innovation in the shape of systematic irrigation. The civilizations of Egypt and Mesopotamia depended heavily upon the two great river systems, the Nile and the Tigris-Euphrates, which both watered the ground with their annual floods and rejuvenated it with the rich alluvium they deposited. The Nile flooded with regularity each summer, and the civilizations building in

In Nazca, Peru, an ancient Incan irrigation canal that uses cut stones is still operational.

its valley early learned the technique of basin irrigation, ponding back the floodwater for as long as possible after the river had receded, so that enriched soil could bring forth a harvest before the floods of the following season. In the Tigris-Euphrates valley the irrigation problem was more complex because the floods were less predictable, were more fierce, and came earlier than those of the northward-flowing Nile. They also carried more alluvium, which tended to choke irrigation channels. The task of the Sumerian irrigation engineers was that of channeling water from the rivers during the summer months, impounding it, and distributing it to the fields in small installments. The Sumerian system eventually broke down because it led to an accumulation of salt in the soil, with a consequent loss of fertility. Both systems, however, depended on a high degree of social control, requiring skill in measuring and marking out the land and an intricate legal code to ensure justice in the distribution of precious water. Both systems, moreover, depended on intricate engineering in building dikes and embankments, canals and aqueducts (with lengthy stretches underground to prevent loss by evaporation), and the use of water-raising devices such as the shadoof, a balanced beam with a counterweight on one end and a bucket to lift the water on the other.

URBAN MANUFACTURING

The manufacturing industry in the early civilizations concentrated on such products as pottery, wines, oils, and cosmetics, which had begun to circulate along the incipient trade routes before the introduction of metals; these became the commodities traded for the metals. In pottery, the potter's wheel became widely used for spinning the clay into the desired shape, but the older technique of building pots by hand from rolls of clay remained in use for some purposes. In the production of wines and oils various forms of press were developed, while the development of cooking, brewing, and preservatives justified the assertion that the science of chemistry began in the kitchen. Cosmetics too were an offshoot of culinary art.

Pack animals were still the primary means of land transport, the wheeled vehicle developing slowly to meet the divergent needs of agriculture, trade, and war. In the latter category, the chariot appeared as a weapon, even though its use was limited by the continuing difficulty of harnessing a horse. Military technology brought the development of metal plates for armor.

BUILDING

In building technology the major developments concerned the scale of operations rather than any particular innovation. The late Stone Age communities of Mesopotamia had already built extensively in sun-dried brick. Their successors continued the technique but extended its scale to construct the massive square temples called ziggurats. These had a core and facing of bricks, the facing walls sloping slightly inward and broken by regular pilasters built into the brickwork, the whole structure ascending in two or three stages to a temple on the summit. Sumerians were also the first to build columns with brick made from local clay,

The pyramids at Giza, Egypt

which also provided the writing material for the scribes.

In Egypt, clay was scarce but good building stone was plentiful, and builders used it in constructing the pyramids and temples that remain today as outstanding monuments of Egyptian civilization. Stones were pulled on rollers and raised up the successive stages of the structure by ramps and by balanced levers adapted from the water-raising shadoof. The stones were shaped by skilled masons, and they were placed in position under the careful supervision of priest-architects who were clearly competent mathematicians and astronomers, as is evident from the precise astronomical alignments. It seems certain that the heavy labor of construction fell upon armies of slaves, which helps to explain both the achievements and limitations of early civilizations. Slaves were usually one of the fruits of military conquest, which presupposes a period of successful territorial expansion, although their status as a subject race could be perpetuated indefinitely. Slave populations provided a competent and cheap labor force for the major constructional works that have been described. On the other hand, the availability of slave labor discouraged technological innovation, a social fact that goes far toward explaining the comparative stagnation of mechanical invention in the ancient world.

TRANSMITTING KNOWLEDGE

In the ancient world, technological knowledge was transmitted by traders, who went out in search of tin and other commodities, and by craftsmen in metal, stone, leather, and the other mediums, who passed their skills to others by direct instruction or by providing models that challenged other craftsmen to copy them. This transmission through intermediary contact was occurring between the

Detail of a wild game trader, 5th century BCE

ancient civilizations and their neighbors to the north and west during the 2nd millennium BCE. The pace quickened in the subsequent millennium, distinct new civilizations arising in Crete and Mycenae, in Troy and Carthage. Finally, the introduction of the technique of working iron profoundly changed the capabilities and resources of human societies and ushered in the Classical civilizations of Greece and Rome.

Chapter 3

TECHNOLOGICAL ACHIEVEMENTS OF GREECE AND ROME

The contributions of Greece and Rome in philosophy and religion, political and legal institutions, poetry and drama, and in the realm of scientific speculation stand in spectacular contrast with their relatively limited contributions in technology. Their mechanical innovation was not distinguished, and, even in the realms of military and construction engineering, in which they showed great ingenuity and aesthetic sensibility, their work represented more a consummation of earlier lines of development than a dramatic innovation. This apparent paradox of the Classical period of the ancient world requires explanation, and the history of technology can provide some clues to the solution of the problem.

THE MASTERY OF IRON

The outstanding technological factor of the Greco-Roman world was the smelting of iron, a technique—derived from unknown metallurgists, probably in Asia Minor, about 1000 BCE—that spread far beyond the provincial frontiers of the Roman Empire. The use of the metal had become general in Greece and the Aegean Islands by the dawn of the Classical period about 500 BCE, and it appears to have spread quickly westward thereafter. Iron ore, long a familiar material, had defied reduction into metallic form because of the great heat required in the furnace to perform the chemical transformation (about 1,535 °C [2,795 °F] compared with the 1,083 °C [1,981 °F] necessary for the reduction of copper ores). To

An example of a Trojan helmet

reach this temperature, furnace construction had to be improved and ways devised to maintain the heat for several hours. Throughout the Classical period these conditions were achieved only on a small scale, in furnaces burning charcoal and using foot bellows to intensify the heat, and even in these furnaces the heat was not sufficient to reduce the ore completely to molten metal. Instead, a small spongy ball of iron—called a bloom—was produced in the bottom of the furnace. This was extracted by breaking open the furnace, and then it was hammered into bars of wrought iron, which could be shaped as required by further heating and hammering. Apart from its greater abundance, iron for most purposes provided a harder and stronger material than the earlier metals, although the impossibility of casting it into molds like bronze was an inconvenience. At an early date some smiths devised the cementation process for reheating bars of iron between layers of charcoal to carburize the surface of the iron and thus to produce a coat of steel. Such case-hardened iron could be further heated, hammered, and tempered to make knife and sword blades of high quality. The very best steel in Roman times was Seric steel, brought into the Western world from India, where it was produced in blocks a few inches in diameter by a crucible process, melting the ingredients in an enclosed vessel to achieve purity and consistency in the chemical combination.

MECHANICAL CONTRIVANCES

Though slight, the mechanical achievements of the Greco-Roman centuries were not without significance. The world had one of its great mechanical geniuses in Archimedes, who devised remarkable weapons to protect his native Syracuse from Roman invasion and applied his powerful mind to such basic mechanical contrivances as the screw, the pulley, and the lever. Alexandrian engineers, such as Ctesibius and Hero, invented a wealth of ingenious mechanical contrivances including pumps, wind and hydraulic organs, compressed-air engines, and screw-cutting machines. They also devised toys and automata such as the aeolipile, which may be regarded as the first successful steam turbine. Little practical use was found for these inventions, but the Alexandrian school marks an important transition from very simple mechanisms to the more complex devices that properly deserve to be considered "machines." In a sense it provided a starting point for modern mechanical practice.

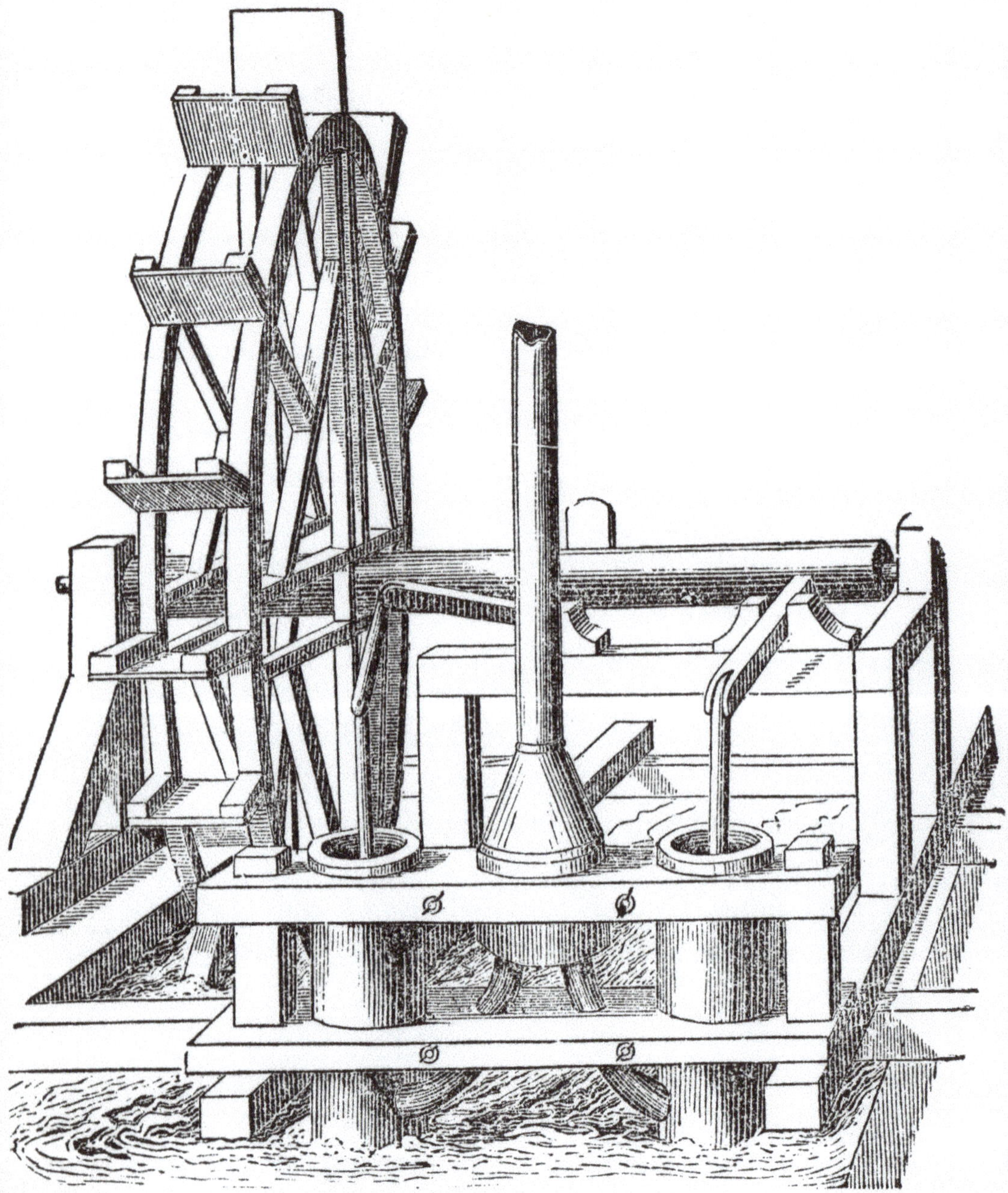

A water-driven pump from the 2nd century BCE designed by Greek inventor Ctesibius

The Romans were responsible, through the application and development of available machines, for an important technological transformation: the widespread introduction of rotary motion. This was exemplified in the use of the treadmill for powering cranes and other heavy lifting operations, the introduction of rotary water-raising devices for irrigation works (a scoop wheel powered by a treadmill), and the development of the waterwheel as a prime mover. The 1st-century-BCE Roman engineer Vitruvius gave an account of watermills, and by the end of the Roman era many were in operation.

BUILDING

Though many buildings of the Greeks survive as splendid monuments to the civilized communities that built them, as technological monuments they are of little significance. The Greeks adopted a form of column and lintel construction that had been used in Egypt for centuries and was derived from experience of timber construction. In no major sense did Greek building constitute a technological innovation. The Romans copied the Greek style for most ceremonial purposes, but in other respects they were important innovators in building technology. They made extensive

A Greek temple, an example of ancient Greek architecture

use of fired brick and tile as well as stone; they developed a strong cement that would set under water; and they explored the architectural possibilities of the arch, the vault, and the dome. They then applied these techniques

in amphitheaters, aqueducts, tunnels, bridges, walls, lighthouses, and roads. Taken together, these constructional works may fairly be regarded as the primary technological achievement of the Romans.

ARCHIMEDES SCREW

One mechanical contrivance was the Archimedes screw, a machine for raising water, allegedly invented by the ancient Greek scientist Archimedes for removing water from the hold of a large ship. One form consists of a circular pipe enclosing a helix and inclined at an angle of about 45 degrees

A 1617 engraving of an Archimedean screw

to the horizontal with its lower end dipped in the water; rotation of the device causes the water to rise in the pipe. Other forms consist of a helix revolving in a fixed cylinder or a helical tube wound around a shaft.

Modern screw pumps, consisting of helices rotating in open inclined troughs, are effective for pumping sewage in wastewater treatment plants. The open troughs and the design of the screws permit the passage of debris without clogging.

OTHER FIELDS OF TECHNOLOGY

In manufacturing, transport, and military technology, the achievements of the Greco-Roman period are not remarkable. The major manufacturing crafts—the making of pottery and glass, weaving, leatherworking, fine-metalworking, and so on—followed the lines of previous societies, albeit with important developments in style. Superbly decorated Athenian pottery, for example, was widely dispersed along the trade routes of the Mediterranean, and the Romans made good quality pottery available throughout their empire through the manufacture and trade of the standardized red ware called terra sigillata, which was produced in large quantities at several sites in Italy and Gaul.

TRANSPORT

Transport, again, followed earlier precedents, the sailing ship emerging as a seagoing vessel with a carvel-built hull (that is, with planks meeting edge-to-edge rather than overlapping

An ancient Egyptian water vessel painted on papyrus

as in clinker-built designs), and a fully developed keel with stempost and sternpost. The Greek sailing ship was equipped with a square or rectangular sail to receive a following wind and one or more banks of oarsmen to propel the ship when the wind was contrary. The Greeks began to develop a specialized fighting ship, provided with a ram in the prow, and the cargo ship, dispensing with oarsmen and relying entirely upon the wind, was also well established by the early years of Classical Greece. The Romans took over both forms, but without significant innovation. They gave much more attention to inland transport than to the sea, and they constructed a remarkable network of carefully

aligned and well-laid roads, often paved over long stretches, throughout the provinces of the empire. Along these strategic highways the legions marched rapidly to the site of any crisis at which their presence was required. The roads also served for the development of trade, but their primary function was always military, as a vital means of keeping a vast empire in subjection.

This drawing shows Gaulish chief Vercingetorix submitting to Julius Caesar after the Battle of Alesia, c. 62 BCE.

Military Technology

Roman military technology was inventive on occasion, as in the great siege catapults, depending on both torsion and tension power. But the standard equipment of the legionnaire was simple and conservative, consisting of an iron helmet and breastplate, with a short sword and an iron-tipped spear. As most of their opponents were also equipped with iron weapons and sometimes with superior devices, such as the Celtic chariots, the Roman military achievements depended more on organization and discipline than on technological superiority. See Chapter 5 for more details.

Chapter 4

AGRICULTURAL TECHNOLOGY

Over time, some plants and animals have become domesticated, or dependent on human interventions for their long-term propagation or survival. Domestication is a biological process in which, under human selection, organisms develop characteristics that increase their utility, as when plants provide larger seeds, fruit, or tubers than their wild progenitors.

Agriculture developed independently in many regions of the world. It was the first profound change in the relationship between fully modern humans and the environment: people evolved into their current form some 200,000–100,000 years ago, yet they did not begin to engage in agriculture until about 15,000–10,000 years before the present.

A cave painting of herdsmen and cattle, from Tassili-n-Ajjer, Algeria

HOW AGRICULTURE AND DOMESTICATION BEGAN

The first agriculture appears to have developed at the closing of the last Pleistocene glacial period, or Ice Age (about 11,700 years ago). At that time temperatures warmed, glaciers melted, sea levels rose, and ecosystems throughout the world reorganized. The changes were more dramatic in temperate regions than in the tropics.

Although global climate change played a role in the development of agriculture, it does not account for the complex and diverse

This fresco depicts agricultural scenes from Egypt's New Kingdom Dynasty XIX, c. 1292 to 1187 BCE.

cultural responses that ensued, the specific timing of the appearance of agricultural communities in different regions, or the specific regional impact of climate change on local environments. By studying populations that did not develop intensive agriculture or certain cultigens, such as wheat and rice, archaeologists narrow the search for causes. For instance, Australian Aborigines and many of the Native American peoples of western North America developed complex methods to manage diverse sets of plants and animals, often including (but not limited to) cultivation. These practices may be representative of activities common in some parts of the world before 15,000 years ago.

The domestication of plants and animals caused changes in their form; the presence or absence of such changes indicates whether a given organism was wild or a domesticate. On the basis of such evidence, one of the oldest transitions from hunting and gathering to agriculture has been identified as dating to between 14,500 and

12,000 BP (before the present) in Southwest Asia. It was experienced by groups known as Epipaleolithic peoples, who survived from the end of the Paleolithic Period into early postglacial times and used smaller stone tools (microblades) than their predecessors.

EARLY DEVELOPMENT

The development of agriculture involves an intensification of the processes used to extract resources from the environment: more food, medicine, fibre, and other resources can be obtained from a given area of land by encouraging useful plant and animal species and discouraging others. As the productivity and predictability of local resources increased, the logistics of their procurement changed, particularly regarding the extent to which people were prepared to travel in order to take advantage of seasonally available items. Group composition eventually became more stable, mobility declined, and, as a consequence, populations increased.

In terms of material culture, durable houses and heavy tools such as pestles, mortars, and grindstones, all of which had long been known, came into more

general use. Although discussions of prehistoric cultures often imply a direct correlation between the development of pottery and the origins of agriculture, this is not a universal

A 1st millenium BCE drawing of a grain grinder from Spain

relationship. In some parts of the Old World, such as Southwest Asia, and in the Americas, pottery appears long after agriculture starts, while in East Asia, where the first pottery dates to as early as 13,700 BP, the opposite is the case.

EARLY AGRICULTURAL SOCIETIES

In the Old World, settled life developed on the higher ground from Iran to Anatolia and the Levant and in China in the semiarid loess plains and the humid Yangtze valley. In contrast, the earliest civilizations based on complex and productive agriculture developed on the alluviums of the Tigris, Euphrates, and Nile rivers. Villages and townships existed in the Euphrates valley in the latter part of the 7th millennium BP. Soon the population was dispersed in hamlets and villages over the available area. Larger settlements provided additional services that the hamlets themselves could not.

SUMER

The land in Sumer (southern Mesopotamia) was cultivated by oxen pulling light plows, and the grain was harvested with sickles in the spring. Wagons had solid wheels with leather

A re-creation of a Sumerian plow

tires held in position by copper nails. They were drawn by oxen or onagers (wild asses) that were harnessed by collars, yokes, and headstalls and controlled by reins and a ring through the nose or upper lip and a strap under the jaw. As many as four animals, harnessed abreast to a central pole, pulled a wagon.

The Nile Valley

In ancient Egypt, agricultural exploitation apparently did not intensify until domesticated animals from Southwest Asia were introduced. By the first quarter of the 7th millennium BP in Al-Fayyum, some villages were keeping sheep, goats, and swine and cultivating emmer, barley, cotton, and flax, which was woven into linen. In this dry climate, village silos consisted of pits lined with coiled basketry; crops were harvested with reaping knives slotted with sharp flints. Elsewhere, at Al-Badari in Upper Egypt, animals were also kept; the fact that dead domesticated animals were wrapped in linen and then buried close to villages may indicate that agriculture was closely associated with some form of religious belief.

Mesoamerica

Villages did not become common in the Americas until the so-called Early Formative period, which began about 3800 BP, after corn was domesticated. Village life was based on the extended family, composed of parents and their children's families, which provided the labor force. Villages were organized into larger territorial units based on ceremonial centers that commonly featured flat-topped pyramids.

Eventually, Formative groups such as the Olmec, known for carving colossal stone heads, developed large prosperous towns. Larger territorial units developed about 2000 BP, and Formative cultures were eventually eclipsed by the Maya, Toltec, and Aztec empires. Food was supplied to these empires' large urban centers by a combination of rain-fed swidden fields (temporary agricultural plots produced by cutting back and burning off vegetative cover) and irrigated tropical lowland field systems.

South America

The long use of swidden agriculture in South America is related to its appropriateness for the tropical lowlands: it helped to maintain local soil fertility and mimicked the diverse tropical ecosystem. Labor-intensive technology was not required. Some researchers have proposed that the nature of tropical lowland ecosystems cannot be understood without acknowledging the long-term presence of swidden agriculture.

Agriculture eventually came to support the Inca empire and other highland South American cultures. The problems of maintaining large populations in the highlands were resolved through an agricultural system supported by terracing, irrigation, and fertilizers.

North America

Some early groups in North America harvested wild grass seeds, separating the grain heads from the stalks by pulling or cutting. The stalks were gathered into sheaves. After harvesting, they burned the grass and then broadcast some of the seeds over the burned area, consuming the rest.

Other groups used a variety of agricultural techniques: crops were grown on alluvium caught behind check dams, low walls built in arroyos to catch runoff from the rains; hillside contour terraces helped conserve soil and water; and bordered gardens and irrigation systems were devised. At Snaketown, a Hohokam site in Arizona, a complex canal system supported a large population. Many canals were at least 2 meters (6.5 feet) deep and 3 meters (10 feet) wide. In the Phoenix area, hundreds of kilometers of canals have been found.

At Poverty Point in the lower Mississippi valley (now Poverty Point National Monument), people built a complex set of geometrically arranged mounds that date to between 3800 and 3400 BP. By 3000 BP the Eastern Agricultural Complex supported a complex socioeconomic system exemplified by cultures such as the Adena and its descendant, the Hopewell. In much of the region, communities became fully sedentary; in addition, pottery had become common, mound complexes began to be built over a wide area, and populations were growing rapidly.

AGRICULTURE IN ANCIENT ASIA

In eastern Asia, a number of advances in agricultural tools, practices and techniques, and the choice of crops themselves led to a great increase in efficiency and productivity. As in other parts of the world, technological improvements in agriculture often had wide-ranging sociopolitical and socioeconomic effects as well.

TOOLS AND TECHNIQUES IN CHINA

The first significant revolution in Chinese agricultural technology occurred when iron agricultural implements became available to the Chinese peasantry. The earliest iron plow found in northern Henan dates from the Warring States period (475–221 BCE) and is a flat V-shaped iron piece that must have been mounted on wooden blades and handles. It was small, and there is no evidence that draft animals were used. Cattle-drawn plows do not appear until the 1st century BCE.

Several improvements and innovations, such as the three-shared plow, the louli (plow-and-sow) implement, and the harrow, were developed subsequently. By the end of the Song dynasty in 1279, Chinese agricultural engineering had reached a high state of development.

The common farmers continued to use these early medieval techniques into modern

A model of a plough used in ancient China

times. Their unfenced fields were cultivated by a wooden plow, with or without a cast-iron share and usually drawn by a water buffalo. Harvesting was by sickle or billhook (a cutting tool consisting of a blade with a hooked point fitted with a handle). Sheaves carried from the field were slung at the ends of a pole across an individual's shoulders. The grain was threshed by beating on a frame of slats or by flails on the ground. Winnowing was accomplished by tossing the grain in the wind. Rice was husked by hand pounding in a mortar or with a hand-turned mill. Irrigation techniques varied. The most common perhaps was a wooden, square-paddle chain pump with a radial treadle operated by foot. Fields were drained by open ditches and diking. Night soil, oil cakes, and ash fertilized the soil.

Over the past millennium, the revolution in Chinese agriculture was not in mechanical or chemical technology but rather in the biological sphere: in crops, cropping systems, and land utilization. Under increasing population pressures, cultivation was forced to become more labor-intensive and also to expand into the sandy loams, the arid hills, and the upper reaches of lofty mountains. Lacking major technological inventions, the Chinese peasant had to expand the area under cultivation by finding suitable crops for inferior land.

Agricultural Techniques in Japan

By 3000–2500 BP, social and technological changes seen at least 500 years earlier in Korea were reaching the southern Japanese archipelago. These included paddy agriculture, bronze, and iron; the transformation produced the Yayoi culture. The Yayoi are known for metallurgy, intensive agriculture, and more-centralized sociopolitical organization. The Itazuke site has evidence of well-engineered drainage systems that were used to maintain paddy fields, and ditches and earthworks served as defensive structures around this and other densely populated communities. Crops included rice, millet, wheat, barley, soybeans, adzuki beans, hops, bottle gourds, peaches, and persimmons.

The Indian Subcontinent

Research indicates two early stages of agricultural development in South Asia. In the earlier stage, dating roughly from 9500 to 7500 BP, agriculture was being established in parts of Pakistan, in the northwesternmost part of the subcontinent. At the ancient site of Mehrgarh, where the earliest evidence has been found, barley was the dominant crop and was apparently supplemented with some wheat. The barley found there is the well-developed domesticate, six-row barley. A small amount of wild barley and two-row domesticated barley have also been recovered, although archaeologists do not think that barley was independently domesticated in this region. Four types of wheat—einkorn, emmer, durum, and bread wheat—have also been found. All had diffused from Southwest Asia, so it is thought that barley probably did so as well. However, the early barley and wheat in Mehrgarh have predominantly small spherical grains, indicating that varieties adapted to local conditions were developed there. No evidence of irrigation has been found. Goats and sheep were also raised at Mehrgarh at this time.

The second stage, dating to about 7000 BP at Mehrgarh, includes evidence of another crop, cotton. It is quite likely a local domesticate. Other important crops with histories in the Indian subcontinent are mung beans (*Vigna radiata*), black gram (*Vigna mungo*), horsegram (*Macrotyloma uniflorum*), and pigeon pea (*Cajanus cajun*), all of which appear after about 5000 BP. Rice is present by about 7000 BP (and possibly earlier), but in this early period its status as a cultigen is unclear; fully domesticated rice and little millet (*Panicum sumatrense*) appear in the archaeological record about 4500 BP. Their appearance coincides closely with significant socioeconomic changes in the subcontinent.

IMPROVEMENTS IN AGRICULTURE IN THE WEST

Crop farming and domestication of animals were well established in western Europe by Roman times. The ground in Roman holdings was prepared with hand tools, hoes, and mattocks, doubtless edged with bronze or iron. There was already emphasis on production of wine and oil for sale, rather than cultivation of cereal crops. Tools included carts, plows and plowshares, yokex, ox harnesses, harrows, manure hampers and baskets, packsaddles and pads, spades, shovels, rakes, scythes, axes, wedges, in addition to overseers, housekeepers, laborers

Ancient agricultural tools from Spain

and animal-specific laborers such as swineherds and shepherds.

Most Roman-era hand tools were similar in shape to their modern counterparts. The wooden plow was fitted with an iron share and, later, with a coulter (cutter). It was usually followed by a man with a mattock who broke up clods and cleared the row so seed would fall into it. The farm included a compost pit where human and animal excrement were placed along with leaves, weeds, and household waste.

Although it was realized that different soils were better suited to some crops than to others, the same piece of land was used for all crops. A specific crop, however, was grown in alternate years in what is known as the two-field, or crop-and-fallow, system. Then as now, wheat was mostly sown in autumn. Barley was a spring-sown crop, as were most others.

The harvest was reaped with a curved sickle, though a short-handled sickle was sometimes used along with a short-handled hooklike implement in the left hand to draw together enough grain to be cut at one stroke. In Gaul a reaper was used, with a cart which had a comblike device that tore off the ears as the vehicle was pushed through the crop. Animals were used to thresh grain. Winnowing was still done by tossing grain in the air when there was a favorable wind to blow away the chaff. Grain was ground with a quern, a hand implement made of two stones, a concave base with a convex upper stone fitted into it.

Little attempt was made at selectively breeding livestock, and little was possible, for most of the animals spent their time at open range or in the woods. Transhumance, or seasonal migration in search of pasture, was normal. A supply of clear water near the grazing ground was necessary. Goats were kept in large herds. Swine were also important. Sows were covered (bred) at 12 to 20 months of age. The bacon produced in Gaul had a reputation for quality; swine also flourished in northern Italy and eastern Spain.

Chapter 5

MILITARY TECHNOLOGY

The earliest evidence for a specialized military technology are the stone walls of Jericho, which date from about 8000 BCE, though when the defenses of Jericho were built, humans already had been using weapons of the hunt for millennia. It is evident that the technical problems of hafting a stone onto a handle were not easily solved. Well-made maces were for a long time few in number and wielded only by champions and rulers. The advent of the mace as a purposely designed offensive weapon opened the door to the conscious innovation of specialized military technology. By the middle of the 3rd millennium BCE, copper was employed in mace heads, yielding higher density and greater crushing power. It represents one of the earliest significant uses of metal for other than ornamental purposes.

4th century BCE Iranian mace head

FROM PRECIOUS METALS TO BASE METALS

The dividing line between the utilitarian and the symbolic in warfare has never been clear and unequivocal. Engineering principles that dictated functional effectiveness were not understood in any systematic fashion. However, materials appear to have been applied to early military purposes as much for

Greek bronze plate armor, 15th century BCE

their presumed mystical or magical properties as for their functional worth.

Metalworking was applied to the production of weaponry as early as, or earlier than, any other economically significant pursuit. Precious metals, with their low melting points and great malleability, were worked first; next came copper—at first pure, then alloyed with arsenic or tin to produce bronze—and then iron. A remarkable phenomenon was the persistence of weaponry made of the soft, rare metals such as gold, silver, and electrum (a naturally occurring alloy of gold and silver) long after mechanically superior materials had become available. For example, helmets and body armor of electrum, which were probably intended for actual use, have been found in Egyptian and Mesopotamian burials dating from the 2nd and 3rd millennia BCE.

ANTIQUITY AND THE CLASSICAL AGE, C. 1000 BCE–CE 400

Perhaps the strongest underlying technological feature of the period was the heavy reliance on human muscle, which contrasted starkly with medieval times, when the application of horse power became a prime ingredient of victory. Mastery of wood and bronze for military purposes reached a level during this period that was seldom, if ever, attained afterward. Military mobility was gained by the use of harnesses and animal power for hauling purposes, though human porters proved just as efficient. Therefore pack animals carried rations, tents, and firewood, and carts were used only for bulky items such as siege engines, while soldiers carried all personal equipment.

Though mainly functional, surviving patterns for the Roman military boot, the caliga, suggest high standards of craftsmanship in leatherworking, and the standards of carpentry displayed on classical ships were almost impossibly high when measured against those of later eras.

DEFENSIVE WEAPONRY

The design and production of individual defensive equipment was restricted by the shape of the human form that it had to protect; at the same time, it placed heavy demands on the smith's skills. The large areas to be protected, restrictions on the weight that a combatant could carry, the difficulty of forging metal into the complex contors required, and cost all conspired to force constant change.

Drawing of a bronze Phrygian-type armor and helmet, 4th century BCE, Italy

Helmets

Forging an integral, one-piece dome of metal capable of covering the entire head was extremely difficult. The Corinthian Greek helmet, a deep, bowl-shaped helmet of carefully graduated thickness forged from a single piece of bronze, probably represented the functional as well as aesthetic apex of the bronze worker's art. Many classical Greek helmets of bronze were joined by a seam down the crown.

Iron helmets followed the evolution of iron mail, itself a sophisticated and relatively late development. The legionnaire of the early Roman Republic wore a helmet of bronze, while his successor in the Empire of the 1st century CE wore one of iron.

Shields

Shields were used for hunting long before military application. The size and composition of shields varied greatly, depending on how it worked with the wearer's armor or weapon. The Greek hoplite acquired his name from the *hoplon*, a convex, circular shield, approximately three feet (90 centimeters) in diameter, made of composite wood and bronze. In the 4th century BCE, the soldier of the Roman Republic,

Figure of an Etruscan warrior, 7th century BCE

who fought primarily with the spear, carried an oval shield, while the later imperial legionnaire, who closed in with a short sword, protected himself with the scutum, a large cylindrical shield of leather-clad wood that covered most of his body.

Body Armor

Padded garments, and perhaps armor of hardened leather, preceded edged metal weapons. Next came small metal plates sewn onto a protective garment. By classical times, breastplates of bronze were commonplace among heavy infantry and elite cavalry. Greaves, defenses for the lower leg, closely followed the breastplate. Defenses for more remote portions of the body were probably not common in field service. Bronze was the most common metal for body defenses well into the Iron Age.

The first practical body armor of iron was mail, made of small rings of iron, typically of one-half-inch diameter or less, linked into a protective fabric. The fabrication of mail was extremely labor-intensive and costly. The earliest mail was made of hand-forged links. Later, armorers used punches of hardened iron to cut rings from sheets. The Roman legionnaire was equipped with a *lorica hamata*, a mail shirt, from a very early date. Mail was extremely

Roman depiction of a 1st-century gladiator in combat

flexible and provided good protection. Its main disadvantage was its weight. In the 1st century CE the legionnaire's mail shirt gave way to a segmented iron torso defense, the *lorica segmentata*.

The *lorica segmentata* heralded the production of practical plate armor on a large scale. Classical plate armor probably provided better protection against smashing and heavy piercing blows, while a shirt of well-made mail covered more of the body and, hence, afforded better protection against slashing blows and missiles.

OFFENSIVE WEAPONRY

One of the most striking facets of ancient military technology is the early date by which individual weapons attained their form and the longevity of early offensive weapons concepts. Some of the weapons of antiquity disappeared or were modified, but with the exception of the halberd and crossbow, virtually every significant pre-gunpowder weapon was known in antiquity.

THE AX

The ax developed from a broad blade mortised into a handle at three points and secured with bindings or rivets. Improvements in armor dictated longer, narrower blades designed primarily for piercing rather than cutting. This led to the development of socketed axes, in which the handle passed through a tubular hole cast in the ax head. Sumerian smiths were casting socketed ax heads with narrow piercing blades by 2500 BCE, while simple mortise-and-tenon hafting was still being used in Egypt 1,000 years later.

The Spear

Early humans probably employed spears of fire-hardened wood, then spearheads of knapped stone. Bronze spearheads followed and were, with the piercing ax, the earliest significant military application of bronze. Spearheads were also among the earliest militarily significant applications of iron. The spears of antiquity were relatively short, commonly less than the height of the warrior, and typically were wielded with one hand. As defensive armor and other weapons of shock combat (notably the sword) improved, spear shafts were made longer. The Greek hoplite's spear was about 9 feet (2.7 m) long; the Macedonian sarissa was twice that length in the period of Alexander's conquests, and it grew to some 21 feet (6.4 m) in Hellenistic times.

The Javelin

Javelins, or throwing spears, were shorter and lighter than spears designed for shock combat and had smaller heads. Javelin troops were commonly used for skirmishing. A throwing string was sometimes looped around the shaft and tied to the thrower's finger to impart spin to the javelin on release. This improved the weapon's accuracy and probably increased the range and penetrating power by permitting a harder cast. Like the spear, the javelin was relatively unaffected by the appearance of iron and retained its characteristic form until it was finally abandoned as a serious weapon in the 16th century.

The Sling

The sling was simple in design, but difficult in practice. It consisted of two cords or thongs fastened to a pouch. A small stone was placed in the pouch, and the slinger whirled the whole affair around to build up velocity before letting go of one of the cord ends to release the projectile. While considerable velocity could be imparted to a projectile in this way, the geometry of the scheme dictated that the release be timed with uncanny precision to achieve even rudimentary accuracy. The sling vanished as a weapon of war in the Old World by the end of the classical period.

THE SWORD

As a serious military implement, the sword had to await the development of iron forging, and the first true swords date from about 1200 BCE. Swords in antiquity and classical times tended to be relatively short, at first because they were made of bronze and later because they were rarely called upon to penetrate iron armor. The blade of the classic Roman stabbing sword, the gladius, was only some two feet (.6 m) long, though in the twilight years of the empire the gladius gave way to the spatha, the long slashing sword of the barbarians.

THE BOW

In its most basic form, the bow consisted of a stave of wood slightly bent by the tension of a bowstring connecting its two ends. The total amount of potential energy that an archer could store in a bow was a function of the bow's length. The longer the arms of the bow, the more kinetic energy imparted to the string and arrow. However long bows had lower velocity, while shorter bows compensated for less stored energy with higher velocity.

Neolithic hunters used simple bows as depicted in cave paintings of 30,000 BCE and earlier. The first improvement was the reflex bow, a bow that was curved forward, or reflexively, near its center so that the string lay close against the grip before the bow was drawn. The next major improvement was the composite recurved bow. The composite bow's resistance to bending was increased by reinforcing the rear, or belly, of the bow with horn; its speed and power in recoil were increased by overlaying the front of the bow with sinew, usually applied under tension. They acquired the name recurved since the outer arms of the bow curved away from the archer when the bow was strung. This bow was used as early as 3000 BCE.

A prime advantage of the composite bow was that it could be engineered to essentially any desired strength.

Arrows

Arrow design was probably the first area of military technology in which the cost of making them was important. As a consequence, the materials used for arrowheads tended to be a step behind those used for other offensive technologies. Arrowheads of flint and obsidian, knapped to remarkably uniform standards,

Bronze statue of an archer from the Sardinia region of Italy

survived well into the Bronze Age, and bronze arrowheads were used long after the adoption of iron for virtually every other military cutting or piercing implement. Arrow shafts were made of relatively inexpensive wood and reed throughout history. Remarkably refined techniques for fastening arrowheads of flint and obsidian to shafts were well in hand long before recorded history.

Mechanical Artillery

Mechanical artillery of classical times was of two types: tension and torsion. In the first, energy to drive the projectile was provided by the tension of a drawn bow; in the other, it was provided by torsional energy stored in bundles of twisted fibers.

The earliest of the Greek engines was the gastrophetes, or "belly shooter." In effect a large crossbow, it received its name because the user braced the stock against his belly to draw the weapon. By the middle of the 3rd century BCE, the bow had been replaced by rigid wooden arms constrained in a wooden box and drawn against the force of tightly twisted bundles of hair or sinew. Such catapults could throw a javelin as far as 800 yards (700 m). The same basic principle was applied to large stone-throwing engines.

RECREATING ANCIENT ARTILLERY

In ancient Greece around 300 BCE, a complex weapon called the polybolos was thought to have been invented by the Greek engineer Dionysius of Alexandria. According to notes and diagrams from the period, the polybolos was a repeating catapult that could shoot multiple arrows in rapid succession automatically. In the surviving diagrams, the weapon is seen to have two pentagonal gears connected by a chain to a type of hoisting winch called a windlass. Arrows could be loaded into a rotating tray, where they would fall into place and activate the automatic trigger through gravity. While there is evidence for the design of the weapon, there are no records of the polybolos actually being used by the ancient Greeks in combat. There is also no evidence that one was ever built.

In 2010, the television show *Mythbusters* attempted to prove if this weapon could have actually functioned as it did on paper. They created a prototype using materials similar to what the Greeks would have used and experienced some initial trouble because the weapon repeatedly broke down. However, after some tinkering, the show makers were able to shoot 15 arrows in under two minutes. They ultimately declared the weapon to be plausible.

The Romans called their catapults onagers, or wild asses, for the way in which their rears kicked upward under the recoil force. The Romans used large ballistae and onagers effectively in siege operations, and a complement of carroballistae, small, wheel-mounted torsion engines, was a regular part of the legion. The onager and the medieval catapult were identical in concept, but ballistae were not used after the classical era.

FORTIFICATION

Fortifications in antiquity were designed primarily to defeat attempts at escalade, though cover was provided for archers and javelin throwers along the ramparts and for fire from flanking towers. Roman fortresses of the 2nd century CE, tended to have square or rectangular outlines and were situated along major communication routes. By the late 3rd century, their walls had become thicker and had flanking towers strengthened to support mechanical artillery. The number of gates was reduced, and the ditches were dug wider. By the late 4th and 5th centuries, Roman fortresses were being built on easily defensible ground with irregular outlines that conformed to the topography; clearly, passive defense had become the dominant design consideration.

Early field fortifications also used topography to their advantage. The Greeks aimed to secure an advantage by standing on higher ground so that the enemy was forced to attack uphill. The Romans were especially adept at

Porta Asinaria, a gate in the fortified Aurelian Walls, Rome

field fortifications, preparing fortified camps at the close of each day's march. The troops usually required three to four hours to dig a ditch around the periphery, erect a rampart or palisade from timbers carried by each man, lay out streets, and pitch tents. During extended campaigns the Romans strengthened the camps with towers and outlying redoubts, or small forts, and used the camps as bases for offensive forays into the surrounding territory.

For breaching fortified positions, military engineers of the classical age designed assault towers that remain a wonder to modern engineers. So large was one siege tower used by Macedonians in an attack on Rhodes that 3,400 men were required to move it up to the city walls. Another 1,000 men were needed to wield a battering ram 180 feet (55 m) long. The Romans constructed huge siege towers, one of which Caesar mentions as being 150 feet (46 m) high. The lower stories housed the battering ram, which had either a pointed head for breaching or a ramlike head for battering. Archers in the upper stories shot arrows to drive the defenders from their ramparts. From the top of the tower, a hinged bridge might be lowered to serve a storming party. To guard the attackers against enemy missiles, the Romans used great wicker or wooden shields, called mantelets, which were sometimes mounted on wheels. In some cases the attackers might approach the fortress under the protection of wooden galleries.

LAND TRANSPORTATION

In antiquity and classical times the transportation technology of land warfare largely amounted to man's own powers of locomotion. The horse was an economically inefficient animal, consuming large quantities of food. Of more importance, keeping and breeding horses was labor-intensive and costly. Mules and donkeys fitted with carrying baskets, or panniers, balanced in pairs across the back, were the most common pack or dray animals. The ox, the heavy-duty dray animal of the Mediterranean world, was used for military purposes when heavy loads were involved and speed was not critical.

The horse was restricted to a subsidiary role in warfare from the eclipse of the chariot in the middle of the 2nd millennium BCE until the rise of the horse archer in the 4th century CE. Greek vase paintings from the 7th century BCE depict tall, apparently powerful horses with long, slender legs, implying speed. Later Mongolian steppe ponies, though tough and tractable, were probably considerably smaller.

The war elephant was first used in India and was known to the Persians by the 4th century BCE. Though they accomplished little subsequently, their presence in Hannibal's army during its transit of the Alps into Italy in 218 BCE underscored their perceived utility. The elephant's tactical importance apparently stemmed in large part from its willingness to charge both men and horses and from the panic that it inspired in horses.

The chariot was the earliest means of transportation in combat. The earliest known chariots, shown in Sumerian depictions from about 2500 BCE, were four-wheeled carts with solid wooden wheels drawn by a team of four donkeys or wild asses. They were no doubt heavy and cumbersome; lacking a pivoting front axle, they would have skidded through turns.

Around 1600 BCE Iranian tribes introduced the war-horse with the light two-wheeled chariot. The Hyksos apparently introduced the chariot into Egypt shortly thereafter, by which time it was a mature technology. By the middle of the 2nd millennium BCE, Egyptian, Hittite, and Palestinian chariots were extraordinarily light and flexible vehicles. Light war chariots were drawn by either two or three horses, which were harnessed by means of chest girths secured by one or two poles and a yoke.

The decline of the chariot by the end of the 2nd millennium BCE was probably related to the spread of iron weaponry, but it was surely related also to the breeding of horses with sufficient strength and stamina to carry an armed man. Chariots lingered in areas of slower technological advance, but in the classical world they were retained mainly for ceremonial functions.

Conclusion

Humankind continues to manipulate the environment and create new technology to reach its collective needs more efficiently. It is impossible to pick one technology that provided the greatest impact on the evolution of humans as each inevitably follows and builds off another. From the use of rocks to arrowheads, humans created ways to provide more meat and then controlled fire to cook it, thus making the proceeds of the kill last longer. Farming and agricultural techniques ended the nomadic lifestyle for many and created towns and cities. Towns and cities begat a new social structure that required architectural advances and later military and defensive ones.

In Europe, the fall of the Romans would eventually lead to the Medieval and Renaissance periods. The former began in the 5th century CE and would continue until the 15th century. These eras brought their own powerful innovations, many of which were improvements or reworkings of Greek and Roman creations, such as the improved windmill and watermill. The 11th and 12th centuries would also herald the use of mills to harness tidal power and the advent of mechanical clocks. Like the all-important wheels that provided a new form of conveyance, the march of technology continues ever forward.

Glossary

amphitheaters Large buildings with curved row seating that rise around a space where games or plays are held.

barbs Sharp projections that extend backward, preventing them from being easily extracted.

breaching Making a hole or opening in something such as a wall or fortification.

campaign Coordinated military operation during war.

cire perdue A process used in metal casting where a wax model surrounded by clay is heated until it drains out of small holes and is then replaced by molten metal.

crucible The vessel in which metals are heated to very high temperatures or melted.

cuneiform A form of writing used in parts of the ancient Middle East.

distilling A process by which a liquid is heated until it becomes gas and then cooled again to make alcohol.

fermenting A process by which food goes through a chemical change to make alcohol.

forged Reshaping of iron by heating it.

hinterland A region that is remote from urban areas.

mail Body armor made of metal links and plates.

metallurgy The study of metals, specifically

dealing with extracting and purifying metals.

Neolithic The latest period of the Stone Age, characterized by polished stone implements.

Paleolithic A period during the early Stone Age when people made rough tools and weapons from stone.

redoubt A small building or area that provides protection to soldiers under attack.

sheaves Stalks and grain that are tied together after being cut.

topography The features of an area of land, such as mountains, plains, and rivers.

ziggurat Ancient Mesopotamian temple tower in the shape of a pyramid with outside staircases and a shrine at the top.

For More Information

American Museum of Natural History
Central Park West at 79th Street
New York, NY 10024-5192
(212) 769-5100
Website: http://www.amnh.org
The American Museum of Natural History boasts a wide selection of artifacts from the ancient world.

Archaeological Institute of America
656 Beacon Street, 6th Floor
Boston, MA 02215-2006
(617) 353-9361
Website: http://www.archaeological.org
The institute is devoted to the field of archaeology. The group organizes activities to promote archaeological inquiry and an appreciation of diverse cultures.

The British Museum
Great Russell Street
London WC1B DG
England
Website: http://www.ancientcivilizations.co.uk/home_set.html
This museum provides online access to an ancient civilizations site that allows users to look at models and objects from the museum's extensive collection.

The California Museum of Ancient Art
P.O. Box 10515
Beverly Hills, CA 90213
(818) 762-5500
The museum includes art and artifacts from the 3rd and 2nd millennia BCE. Its collection includes pieces from ancient Egypt, Mesopotamia, and the Holy Land.

Canadian Museum of History
100 Laurier Street
Gatineau, QB K1A 0M8
Canada
(800) 555-5621
Website: http://www.historymuseum.ca
This museum focuses on Canadian and world history and includes resources for those studying archaeology, ethnology, and cultural studies. The museum has a large collection of artifacts from the ancient world.

Metropolitan Museum of Art
1000 5th Avenue
New York, NY 10028
(212) 535-7710
Website: http://www.metmuseum.org
This museum has a large collection of items from the ancient world including artifacts from ancient Egypt and examples of Greco-Roman art, technology, and weaponry.

For Further Reading

Bard, Kathryn A. *An Introduction to the Archaeology of Ancient Egypt*. Hoboken, NJ: Wiley-Blackwell, 2015.

Brooks, Philip. *Ancient Civilizations: Discovering the People and Places of Long Ago*. Helotes, TX: Armadillo, 2015.

D'Amato, Raffaele. *Republican Roman Warships 509-27 BC*. Oxford, England: Osprey Publishing, 2015.

Evans, John. *Ancient Stone Implements, Weapons, and Ornaments of Great Britain*. New York, NY: Cambridge University Press, 2015.

Fara, Patricia. *Science: A Four Thousand Year History*. New York, NY: Oxford University Press, 2010.

Headrick, Daniel R. *Technology: A World History.* New York, NY: Oxford University Pres, 2009.

Hood, Jane. *How to Win a Roman Chariot Race: Lives, Legends and Treasures from the Ancient World*. London, England: Icon Books, Ltd., 2015.

National Geographic Concise History of Science and Invention: An Illustrated Timeline. Washington, DC: National Geographic, 2009.

Smith, Amanda, and Philip Steele. *Ancient Worlds: A Thrilling Adventure Through the Ancient Worlds*. London, England: Kingfisher, 2016.

Usher, Abbott Payson. *A History of Mechanical Inventions*. New York, NY: Dover Publications, 2011.

Index